Written by Natasha Kate Evans and Illustrated by Anthony Princi

Copyright © 2016 Natasha Kate Evans

The moral right of the author has been asserted.

Apart from any fair dealing for the purposes of research or private study, or criticism or review, as permitted under the Copyright, Designs and Patents Act 1988, this publication may only be reproduced, stored or transmitted, in any form or by any means, with the prior permission in writing of the publishers, or in the case of reprographic reproduction in accordance with the terms of licences issued by the Copyright Licensing Agency. Enquiries concerning reproduction outside those terms should be sent to the publishers.

This work of fiction is based on a true story.

Matador
9 Priory Business Park,
Wistow Road, Kibworth Beauchamp,
Leicestershire. LE8 0RX
Tel: 0116 279 2299
Email: books@troubador.co.uk
Web: www.troubador.co.uk/matador
Twitter: @matadorbooks

ISBN 978 1785892 158

British Library Cataloguing in Publication Data.
A catalogue record for this book is available from the British Library.

Matador is an imprint of Troubador Publishing Ltd

# DYLAN JAMES TOMBIDES
8th March 1994 – 18th April 2014

In memory of a true champion.

*"You can't tell me the sky's the limit when there are footprints on the moon"*

# Foreword

As Vice-Chairman of West Ham United Football Club, I am very proud that Dylan wore our famous Claret and Blue. My board and I cherish the longstanding relationship with his wonderful family and his namesake charity, the DT38 Foundation.

Dylan was a very special young man who had a profound effect on those around him at the Club. His fortitude in the face of the illness that ultimately took his life was amazing and we're humbled to be working with DT38.

A hugely popular figure among his team-mates, coaches, backroom staff, supporters and opponents alike, Dylan was loved and respected throughout the football community for his talent, his smile and his spirit. Dylan was already a star, we all knew it. What he achieved in his twenty years was astonishing, but we also knew that he had the potential to go on and accomplish even greater things. This book will ensure that the stars of the future have the opportunity that Dylan, tragically, was robbed of: to fulfil their potential.

Though Dylan, sadly, left us, his legacy will always live on at West Ham and far beyond. I know Dylan's mother, Tracylee, works tirelessly to honour his memory in the very best way possible, as a force for good.

Dylan's considerable legacy is now channelled through DT38, which raises testicular cancer awareness through education and opportunity. It's astonishing what the Tombides family have achieved in so little time and I'm sure Dylan would be very proud indeed. Although the Foundation is still in its infancy, it is already going from strength to strength and we will continue to support a truly worthy cause.

At West Ham, we take great pride in taking care of our own. Dylan and his family will always be part of the West Ham family. Dylan's No38 shirt, now formally retired by the Club, will forever stand as a mark of respect to a young man with so much to give.

We thought the world of Dylan and I know how much he loved West Ham United.

Use this book to help inspire you to work hard to achieve your future hopes and dreams.

*West Ham United Vice-Chairman Baroness Brady*

Written by Natasha Kate Evans

and

Illustrated by Anthony Princi

When Didge and Roo were born, their parents, Jimbo and Trace, knew that two very special animals had entered the world. They were nurtured and loved by their family and they were always surrounded by family and friends. Their parents taught them many important life lessons that they could use in their future years.

Didge loved his family and friends but he developed a love like no other for something else: football!

Didge's love for the round ball grew stronger by the day. When he was old enough, his father Jimbo enrolled him into his local football club.

Jimbo shared the same passion for football as his son and he was Didge's first coach. Jimbo was the proudest lion in town to have the opportunity to teach his little cub about the game he also adored so much.

Didge met many different types of animals in his team. There were kangaroos, roosters, tigers, elephants, monkeys, echidnas and even tortoises. Didge got on with everyone, no matter what type of animal they were. When the tortoise was slow, Didge would be the one to encourage him not to give up; when the tiger got angry, Didge would be the one to calm him down. He was a born leader and he made sure he shared his skills with those around him.

Within no time, Didge had an abundance of friends, but one friend was particularly special – his brother Roo. Didge and Roo always got up to mischief together. As an older brother, Didge knew the importance of guiding his little brother and he did this job with great loyalty and pride.

As Didge grew older he started to think more about his future dreams and aspirations. Didge and his friends would often meet up and at one of their meetings he told them all that one day he would play football on the world stage.

Didge knew that he wouldn't be able to do this without hard work and dedication. He spent a lot of his time training at his field of dreams, 'The Den.' It was here that a wise owl not only noticed Didge's football talent, but also his charismatic charm, smile and beautiful nature: all the qualities of a true champion.

Jimbo and Trace always wanted the best for their boys. One thing they wanted them to do was to explore the world and learn about other amazing animals that roamed the earth. The boys left Perth, Australia but they were excited for the many adventures that awaited them.

The wise owl always kept in touch with Didge and his family as they embarked on their journey to different parts of the world. He knew a powerful bulldog that lived in London. The owl made the bulldog aware of Didge's many talents.

This made the bulldog very intrigued. He told the wise owl, "Bring him to me immediately!" And before you knew it Didge and his family moved to London, United Kingdom.

This bulldog was the coach of Didge's favourite English football team and he wanted Didge to join his team at a very young age. Didge couldn't believe it – all of his dreams were coming true!

Didge continued to train hard and he made many new friends in London but he continued to keep in touch with his friends back in Perth because he missed them very much. Every time he heard a 'cock-a-doodle-do' he would think of his mate Robbie the Rooster. Didge sure missed Curt the Elephant, but he definitely didn't miss the splashing water from Curt's extraordinarily large trunk all over his perfectly groomed mane. Benny the Bird would fly himself and Didge's closest friends to London at least once a year to visit him.

One day Didge was busy training when his extremely excited coach called him over for a chat. He had some incredible news: the head of the Australian football team wanted Didge to go to Mexico to play in the World Cup! Didge played the tournament of his life and scored an unbelievable goal that captured the attention of the world.

After the tournament, Didge noticed a bite mark on his leg. Sena the sneaky, slithering snake had bitten him during the game. He must've been jealous of Didge's beautiful mane, not to mention his unique football skills. Sena's venom was terribly poisonous and Didge started to feel very unwell.

When Didge felt a bit better he returned to London. He continued to work hard at his football. Little did he know, Sena had followed him back from the football tournament. He would appear when Didge least expected it. He would often find traces of Sena's skin, which would shed every time he attacked. Sena was so sly that he would attack Didge while he was sleeping.

Each time Sena bit Didge he would become weaker. Trace made it her mission to find something to help her son. She searched the fields far and wide until she came across a mystical house called 'Misty's magical medicines'. Misty the Mouse gave Trace some of her special magic potion and told her to use it wisely as she didn't have much left. Trace gave the potion to Didge immediately and it helped him to feel better.

When Didge felt better he would get straight back to doing what he loved: playing football. He also made it his mission to spread the news about what Sena was doing to him. He realised that he wasn't the only animal that Sena was trying to poison so he tried to help the other animals around him. Didge asked his mum to share the magic potion with them and he made many special friends who were eternally grateful to him and his family.

Sena was disappointed that his venom wasn't as powerful as he thought, so he suddenly disappeared. Didge's positive and persistent attitude allowed him to return to playing football again. During this time Didge taught Roo some of his special football tricks and told him that they would help him become the best player he could be. Jimbo and Trace were so proud to see the everlasting love their sons had for each other.

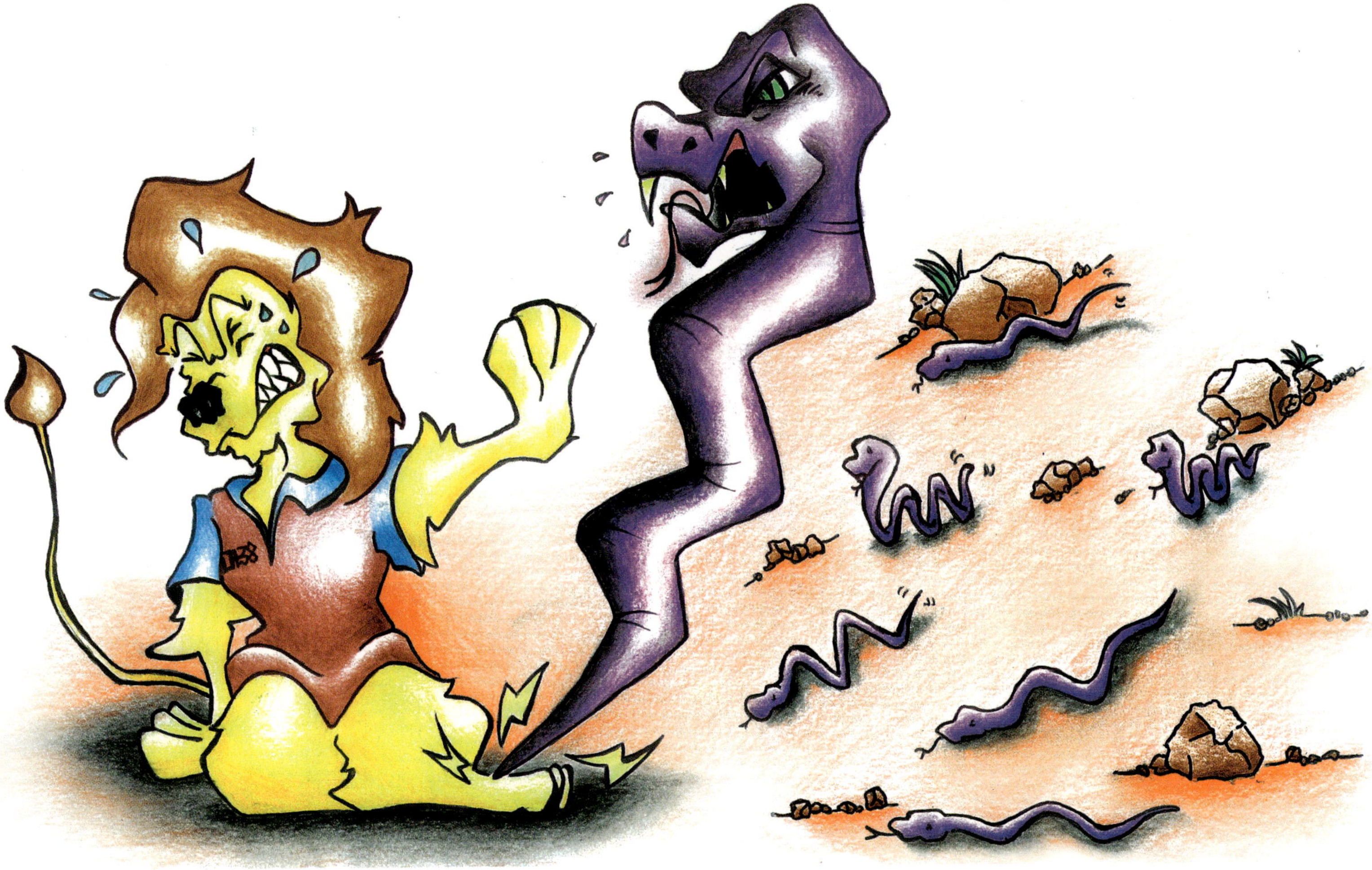

Right when Didge thought Sena had gone forever he returned with an army of snakes. They struck as fast as a lightning bolt and Didge's body became riddled with venom. His family tried to give him the magic potion but this time the venom was too poisonous.

Didge's family were so upset! They felt helpless as there was nothing more they could do. Didge told them that he had a plan! "Mum, you're a dove and you can fly. If you fly me high enough in the sky, I will start my own kingdom. It can be a place where other animals can be protected from hurtful animals like Sena."

Didge's family didn't want him to start his own kingdom but they were so proud that their little cub had grown into a strong and courageous lion. They knew it was the only way he could escape the pain Sena had caused him.

Before Didge left, he told his brother Roo something really important. "Roo, we were blessed with many gifts. Remember all of the special things I taught you. Go and show the world what you're made of. I will watch over you every step of the way."

His father Jimbo was so honoured and grateful to know that he raised such an inspirational lion.

Just like when he was born, his mother carried her son in her wings. She took him to the sky.

Didge promised her that he would always look down upon his family and friends. He asked them to spread the word about his life to those on Earth while he started building his new kingdom.

# BEING DYLAN

By Tracylee Tombides

8th March 1994 was the day Dylan James Tombides entered the world. He was raised in Perth, Western Australia and being Dylan meant that he never went anywhere without a ball. He went to bed with a ball, to the playground with a ball and even to sleep with a ball. Dylan played his first competitive match as a five-year-old for Wembley Downs Soccer Club and never looked back. He loved his sport and he would always play football. In the off seasons he played basketball, cricket, teeball, tennis and indoor soccer.

At the age of eleven, Dylan moved to Stirling Lions and played there for one season before joining Perth SC. In 2007, Dylan and his family moved to live in Macau and the football continued, although it was nothing like back home. He still trained on grass pitches, but he played on artificial ones too with older boys and young men. He played in cages on concrete and he played on rooftops. He had a hunger for the game and every weekend he would sail to Hong Kong to train Friday night, play Saturday morning and train with Coerver on Saturday afternoon before returning.

In 2008, Dylan joined West Ham United and he flourished. He was scoring many goals in the Under 16's and quickly found himself playing in the Under 18's and the reserves and being in and around the first team. Dylan was on a high having spent his 17th birthday with the first team in Portugal where he won the crossbar challenge and made a commercial. He came back to England and continued to shine.

In April 2011, at the age of seventeen, Dylan found a lump in his testicle. He didn't say anything straight away because he had no pain or discomfort. He was playing so much football that when he did start to feel pain and discomfort he put it down to all his exercise. When the pain became a little more consistent Dylan went to his GP. His GP informed him that he had a cyst and that there was nothing to worry about as many people live with cysts. So Dylan continued on with his feeling of being on top of the world. He finished the Barclays Premier League season on the bench for the first team against Sunderland at the end of May and then travelled to Australia four days later to join up with his Aussie teammates to prepare for the Under 17's World Cup in Mexico. While in Mexico, Dylan caught the eye of Nike and he was offered a five-year contract but on the last game of the tournament for Australia, Dylan had a random drugs test and the results came back positive for a tumour.

Dylan was finally diagnosed with testicular cancer three months after his initial GP consultation. Dylan fought very hard to maintain his fitness and strength while going through chemotherapy. He amazed everyone with his determination and his constant smile and banter. He once described himself as the happiest kid with cancer. But his cancer would not go away.

Every time Dylan had treatment six to eight weeks later it would return. It returned stronger and more resilient than before. In January 2012, he had surgery to remove his lymph nodes called RPLND, but by June his cancer returned. Amid Dylan's brave battle came his brightest day, his senior West Ham United debut on 25th September 2012. Dylan replaced Gary O'Neil in the 84th minute of a third round Capital One Cup tie with Wigan Athletic. Though the Hammers lost 4-1, it was a moment that Dylan would never forget. The culmination of a life-time's determination and desire, a dream come true.

In December 2012, Dylan had high dose chemotherapy and stem cell transplants twice within eight weeks. In March 2013, Dylan was preparing for the Under-20 World Cup and his cancer resurfaced in his liver. He had to have his liver resected and was out for the next three months.

During this time, Dylan went into the club every day and worked on his banter, his snooker game and the exercise bike. He continued to do mild exercise until he was allowed to do more physical training. Dylan had a couple of minor procedures throughout July and October and in November 2013 Dylan's cancer returned again.

He was determined to have his three-week course of Chemotherapy and be fit for the Under 22 tournament in Oman in January 2014. Dylan completed his course of chemotherapy and played for Australia in January but by the time he returned three weeks later, Dylan's cancer had not responded to the treatment and the doctors said that they could no longer offer Dylan a cure. Dylan travelled to Germany where they offered hope and treatments not available in the UK. Dylan stayed strong throughout his next phase of treatment but Dylan's cancer was rare and he had had so much chemotherapy that they were worried that his organs would fail.

On the 18th April 2014, Dylan's organs failed and we said goodbye to our beloved son and brother. His West Ham family thought so highly of him they retired his number 38 shirt. It breaks our heart to think that this could have been prevented. If we had known about testicular cancer and what we needed to do to catch it early we would have insisted on an ultrasound when we went to the GP. Dylan was robbed of a future that he dreamed of as a young boy. It robbed Taylor of a brother and it robbed my husband and I of watching our beautiful son growing and fulfilling his dreams.

If you have a concern with your testicles please see a doctor straight away and insist on an ultrasound – it may just save your life! Please don't let this happen to your sons, your brothers or your fathers.

We miss you so, Dylan. You have left a void that no one can fill.

In December 2012, Dylan had high dose chemotherapy and stem cell transplants twice within eight weeks. In March 2013, Dylan was preparing for the Under-20 World Cup and his cancer resurfaced in his liver. He had to have his liver resected and was out for the next three months.

During this time, Dylan went into the club every day and worked on his banter, his snooker game and the exercise bike. He continued to do mild exercise until he was allowed to do more physical training. Dylan had a couple of minor procedures throughout July and October and in November 2013 Dylan's cancer returned again.

He was determined to have his three-week course of Chemotherapy and be fit for the Under 22 tournament in Oman in January 2014. Dylan completed his course of chemotherapy and played for Australia in January but by the time he returned three weeks later, Dylan's cancer had not responded to the treatment and the doctors said that they could no longer offer Dylan a cure. Dylan travelled to Germany where they offered hope and treatments not available in the UK. Dylan stayed strong throughout his next phase of treatment but Dylan's cancer was rare and he had had so much chemotherapy that they were worried that his organs would fail.

On the 18th April 2014, Dylan's organs failed and we said goodbye to our beloved son and brother. His West Ham family thought so highly of him they retired his number 38 shirt. It breaks our heart to think that this could have been prevented. If we had known about testicular cancer and what we needed to do to catch it early we would have insisted on an ultrasound when we went to the GP. Dylan was robbed of a future that he dreamed of as a young boy. It robbed Taylor of a brother and it robbed my husband and I of watching our beautiful son growing and fulfilling his dreams.

If you have a concern with your testicles please see a doctor straight away and insist on an ultrasound – it may just save your life! Please don't let this happen to your sons, your brothers or your fathers.

We miss you so, Dylan. You have left a void that no one can fill.

The DT38 foundation has been established and is something Dylan himself would've supported in years to come.

Our vision is to change the way testicular cancer is diagnosed by implementing best practice diagnostic guidelines for patients who present with testicular symptoms. We also aim to arm future generations of young men with the necessary knowledge about testicular cancer that will enable them to be confident when taking health matters into their own hands.

Our mission is to raise awareness and change the stigma associated with men's health issues with a focus on testicular cancer. We aim to do this through providing educational programmes and opportunities for the youth of our community, to help shape a generation of children who are self-aware about their health and wellbeing.

Our main goals are to:
Drive the SELF-AWARENESS campaign for the early detection of testicular cancer
Focus on youth EDUCATION through various teaching programmes aligned to national curriculum
Provide OPPORTUNITIES linked to fun and accessible activities within the community

Please visit www.dt38.org to retrieve further information about the foundation.

Delay
Is
Deadly
Get
Educated

Visit Didge's Kingdom at

www.dt38.org

Follow Didge on Instagram

@didgeskingdom

## Jane Clarke
*Nutritionist*
BSc (Honours) SRD

I sincerely hope that this great, passionately written book informs and inspires the next generation of professionals to positively take an active role in recognising when someone's body needs early treatment. Dylan was a huge inspiration to all who knew him and I count myself to be one of the lucky ones in life to have been within this group, so let all that Tracy, family and friends are campaigning for be a testament to his incredible life…

Dylan's nutritionist
David Beckham's Personal Dietitian & Nutritionist during the 2006 World Cup
Trained Cordon Bleu Chef
Author – Her series of 'Jane Clarke's Bodyfoods' books have all become UK bestsellers and include: *Bodyfoods For Women, Bodyfoods For Life, Bodyfood For Busy People, The Bodyfoods Cookbook*

Jane is a regular contributor on British Television including all major networks- ITV, Channel 4, BBC News and News Night. She was the Nutritional Consultant working alongside Jamie Oliver, on his groundbreaking television series *Jamie's School Dinners* and Jamie's co presenter on *Eat to save your life!* Jane is a regular commentator on nutritional matters for numerous radio shows and stations including Radio 4's *Woman's Hour, PM, The Today Programme* and *Last Word*. Radio 4's *Case Notes* and *The Food Program*, Radio 5 Live *Lively Discussion Programs*, her own *Archive Hour* on Radio 4

## Dr Richard Weiler
*Consultant Physician in Sport & Exercise Medicine*
MBChB FFSEM (UK) MSc SEM MRCGP PGCME FHEA

Dylan had endless positive thoughts, a huge sense of fun, massive ambition and a monstrously cheeky smile, even and especially when he was suffering most. He carried those around him on his wave with a love of life, love for football and successful determination to pursue his dreams, which was defiant, incredible and remarkable. Dylan was unsquashable. This book shares his story and will go a long way to realising Dylan's dream to help prevent others from having to go through his battles.

Club Doctor, West Ham United Football Club
Lead Medical Officer, England and Team GB Disability Football, The Football Association
Honorary Consultant, University College London Hospitals
Lecturer and Module leader, UCL Institute of Orthopaedics, The Royal National Orthopaedic Hospital
Lecturer and external tutor, UCL Institute of Sport, Exercise and Health
Board Member, The Institute of Sports Medicine
Fellows Board, Map of Medicine
Macmillan Cancer Physical Activity Expert Advisory Group
International Olympic Committee Working Party on non-communicable chronic diseases
Patron, Wheelchair Dance Sport Association
Author